LONGBOARDING

MARY-LANE KAMBERG

rosen publishing's
rosen central

For Clayton Phillips

Published in 2017 by The Rosen Publishing Group, Inc.
29 East 21st Street, New York, NY 10010

Copyright © 2017 by The Rosen Publishing Group, Inc.

First Edition

Library of Congress Cataloging-in-Publication Data

Names: Kamberg, Mary-Lane, 1948-
Title: Longboarding / Mary-Lane Kamberg.
Description: First Edition. | New York : Rosen Central, 2017. | Series:
  (Skateboarding Tips and Tricks) | Includes bibliographical references,
  webography and index. | Audience: Grades: 7-12.
Identifiers: LCCN 2016008902| ISBN 9781499438079 (Library Bound) | ISBN
  9781477788639 (Paperback) | ISBN 9781477788646 (6-pack)
Subjects: LCSH: Skateboarding--Juvenile literature.
Classification: LCC GV859.8 .K35 2017 | DDC 796.22--dc23
LC record available at http://lccn.loc.gov/2016008902

Manufactured in China

CONTENTS

INTRODUCTION

In the 1950s in Oahu, Hawaii, kids heard the call and raced to the beach. They paddled out to sea on bulky surfboards, caught a wave, and rode it in to shore. But on days when the surf was low or too rough, they had nothing fun to do—no way to practice their balancing skills or build their endurance.

Until, one day someone strapped two sets of metal roller skate wheels to a wooden board. The "skateboard" let a rider "surf" on the sidewalk using the same motions on land that surfers used on water,

Sidewalk surfing was born. The sport first caught on with surfers in Hawaii and along the West Coast of the United States. Soon teens all across the country built their own boards and joined in. They left the sidewalks and rode on the street.

The first manufactured skateboards, made of wood or fiberglass, hit the toy market in 1959. However, they were too short for teens. Not to be left out, teens made their own with longer pieces of wood and called them longboards. The trouble was the homemade boards weren't very safe. In fact, the risk of injury caused the sport to nearly die out during the 1960s. Interest picked up again in the 1970s thanks to better materials and safety equipment. Clay wheels replaced metal ones. Later, urethane replaced clay. The result was a faster ride.

By the 1990s interest surged due in part to pro skater Tony Hawk. He made doing tricks popular among skateboard riders. Longboarding also attracted a new group of athletes. Snowboarders moved to longboards during warm months.

Today, both skateboarding and longboarding have grown. Longboarding is also being considered for the 2020 Olympic Games in Tokyo. Some riders have even gone pro. To learn more about longboarding, search the Internet for advice on choosing equipment. Look, too, for tutorial videos to learn various tricks. You can also visit manufacturers' websites for more information.

Longboarding is an exciting and unique offshoot of classic skateboarding.

CHAPTER ONE

GEARING UP

Today's well-designed high-performance longboards offer a smoother, longer ride and better turning ability than traditional skateboards. Longboarding includes many different styles of riding, which may overlap. The first is the traditional cruising mainly used for transportation to and from school or work. An outgrowth of this style is the trek or long-distance ride. Riders who love a high-speed experience prefer downhill or freeriding. Still others favor freestyle riding and dancing, which focus on performing tricks during the ride.

Longboards can be custom-made to the rider's wishes depending on the type of ride he or she wants. Longboards share the same basic parts: decks, trucks, and wheels. The differences depend on how the board will be used. Riders can customize theirs for different styles as well as for their body weight. Before choosing a skateboard, determine how you'll use it. A board for downhill racing differs from a board for freestyle riding or transportation. Be sure to try out a friend's (or several friends') board(s) before buying one yourself.

Today's skateboards are safer and offer a smoother ride thanks to better materials and the ability to build a board according to how it will be used. However, riders still need proper safety equipment and gear to prevent or reduce the risk of harm from falls.

DECKS

The deck is the part the rider stands on. It is typically made of sturdy wood such as birch or maple. Manufacturers also use exotic materials like koa, a native Hawaiian tree, and bamboo, a grass that is stronger than wood. Decks may also contain layers of fiberglass, foam cores, carbon fiber, or other composite materials.

Longboards of varying sizes and styles hang in a shop. Some longboards let you go extremely fast.

Decks range from about 35 inches to 50 inches (89 to 127 centimeters) long and 8.5 inches to 10 inches (22 to 25 cm) wide. However, some come shorter than regular skateboards, which typically fall between 28 inches to 32 inches (71 to 81 cm) long and 7.5 to 8.25 inches (19 to 21 cm) wide.

TRUCKS

Longboard trucks are the axles. An axle is a bar that attaches to the center of a wheel and lets it spin. The truck should be within about 0.25 inches (0.64 cm) of the width of the deck. A little too wide is better than a little too narrow. A kingpin is the bolt that holds the truck together. The two types of trucks are standard kingpin (SKP) trucks and reverse kingpin (RKP) trucks. SKP trucks are most commonly used for skateboarding. Longboarders prefer the RKP type. RKP trucks are responsive at slow speed and give more stability and control at high speed. They are best for carving, transportation, freestyle, freeride, and downhill.

Bushings are urethane support cushions in the truck. The shape and hardness affect different riding styles, as does the weight of the rider. Shapes include short cone, tall cone, barrel, eliminator or stepped barrel, and stepped or freeride cone. Hardness is measured on a durometer scale. The softer the durometer, the easier it is to turn the board. The harder the durometer, the more stable the board, which is best for high-speed riding.

WHEELS

Durometer, often called "duro," also measures the hardness of longboard wheels. The durometer of the wheels also affects the ride. The higher the number, the harder the wheel. The durometer scale is a standard "A" scale. Skateboarders generally choose hard wheels with a durometer between 90A and 100A. Longboarders usually prefer softer wheels with a durometer between 75A and 85A. The most common is 78A.

THE ART OF FALLING

You're zinging down a sidewalk on your longboard and hit a crack. *SPLAT!* You're on the ground. Even experienced longboarders take a tumble now and then, but beginners fall more often. So learn how to fall before taking to the streets. Whether you walk away clean or with a bruise, scrape, or broken bone depends on how you land. Here's how to minimize injury:

- **Wear safety equipment that includes a helmet, wrist guards, and knee and elbow pads. They'll absorb some of the force of a fall.**
- **Don't fall on your hands. Even though it's probably your first instinct, you'll risk a broken wrist. Or two.**
- **Don't fall on your elbows. If your**

While longboards seem more stable because of their size, don't get overconfident when you ride them.

(continued on the next page)

(continued from the previous page)

elbow gets the force of the blow, you might break it, too.

- **Hug yourself. Fall with hands and elbows wrapped around your torso.**
- **Fall onto your back and shoulders.**
- **Practice on your lawn. Find a soft place to land and practice falling skills there before you need to use them on pavement.**

Bearings make the wheels spin. As with all other longboard parts, bearings can be sold separately. They use the ABEC rating system for dimensions, tolerances, and noise standards. ABEC 3 and ABEC 5 are most commonly used for longboards.

For more information about the right longboard setup, visit skateboard equipment manufacturers' websites. Many offer tips and advice to help you make your decisions.

SAFETY GEAR

Having fun and challenging yourself on a longboard carry risk of injury. You can prevent or minimize potential harm by wearing protective gear.

Most important: wear a helmet. Whether local laws require helmets or not, concrete is stronger than your skull. Protect your brain! The three main types of helmets are the half-shell, full-cut, and full-face. The half-shell covers the top and back of the head and is the most common type skateboarders use. The full-cut helmet also covers the top and back of the head, as well as the ears. This type of helmet was first used in such water sports as kayaking and wake skating. It has found its way to skaters on land. The full-face helmet covers the entire head and jaw. It protects the chin as well as the skull. Some come with clear face shields. Full-face helmets are recommended for high-speed downhill longboarding. They are required for professional downhill racing.

In addition to helmets, longboarders need knee, elbow, and wrist pads. They offer splint support in case of injury, and many contain foam or other padding materials to absorb the shock of

Longboarders Si Si Zhou (*left*) and Morrah Cameron slide their boards to a perpendicular position to slow down. Both are members of Canada's Toronto Girls Longboarding, founded in 2005.

a fall. Knee pads come in soft-shell and hard-shell types. Soft-shell pads usually slip on over the foot and are pulled up the leg to cover the knee. Users must remove shoes before putting them on. Hard-shell ones wrap around the knee and close in back with what is often called a butterfly closure. In addition, some riders like to wear knee gaskets. Knee gaskets are extra pads worn under the knee pads for extra cushion.

Finally, sliding gloves are important for hands-down sliding. To slide, a rider spins the longboard sideways instead of pointing it in the direction of travel. The skill often involves placing the hands on the street—thus, the need for protective gloves. Sliding is a way to slow down or stop, as well as a way longboarders take corners and generally enhance the ride in downhill and freestyle skating. Some riders make their own sliding gloves by gluing cut-up kitchen cutting boards to garden gloves. Sliding gloves are also available from manufacturers. Some come with foam pucks to protect the palm and Kevlar fingertips and thumb ends.

Wearing safety gear doesn't guarantee you won't get hurt. Skating carelessly or trying to learn new tricks without proper instruction can still be dangerous. And accidents happen. However, the right protection will keep your chances of serious injury as low as possible.

CHAPTER TWO

TAKIN' IT TO THE STREETS

All the longboarding safety gear in the world can't guarantee protection from others who share the road. That includes fellow longboarders, as well as motor vehicles. Crashing into another rider can hurt or injure you both. Communication is key when riding with a friend or in a pack. Develop hand signals that you and your friends agree on. Use these signals to let other riders know when you plan to move, slow down, turn, slide, or change direction.

Vocal signals also work if you are close enough to the other person and traffic noise won't drown you out. A simple "on your left" or "behind you" will prevent your surprising the rider. You'll help avoid sudden movements that can cause a fall or rider-rider collision. Warn your friend if you want to move to the other side of the road. An unexpected action on your part could force him or her into a ditch—or into traffic.

Be aware of your surroundings. Notice the type of road you're on and whether it runs uphill or down. Is it a one-way street, or does traffic run in both directions? And no matter how much you might enjoy listening to tunes while you ride, leave your headphones at home. You need to be able to hear potential dangers at all times.

Use bike lanes when possible. But, stay far enough away from curbs to avoid sticks, leaves, rocks, and trash that can collect there. Other hazards include vehicles parked in the bike lane, car doors opening, and drivers making U-turns. Train tracks, manhole covers, potholes, and other pavement flaws pose additional challenges.

LOOK OUT FOR CARS

Once you're on the street, you're considered a vehicle. Obey stop signs and signals, turn lanes, no U-turn postings, and other rules of the road. Ride defensively. Watch out for inattentive drivers and those who ignore traffic laws. However, remember that you and your board are smaller than big, heavy motor vehicles. In a crash, you'll be hurt worse than the car or truck. In short, don't run into one.

Avoid sudden movements that car drivers don't expect. And be sure you can be seen at night. Wear reflective clothing or lights that attach to helmets or clothes.

Corners and curves can pose difficulties. If you're turning left at a corner, stay to the right to keep from running off the road. If turning right, take care not to drift into the oncoming lane of traffic.

A blind corner is one where shrubbery, signs, slope, or other obstructions prevent viewing the new side of the street. Hairpin curves pose the same risk. Neither the rider nor an oncoming driver can see what's ahead. Drifting into the wrong lane in these circumstances can have serious consequences. The safest

Longboardiing down roads in hiilly or even mountainous terrain can be thrilling due to the speeds you can achieve, but it can be equally frightening because the potential for injury is great, too.

practice is to use a spotter to alert you to potential perils on the blind side of the corner or curve. Alternate being the rider and spotter so you both enjoy the ride.

Know the posted speed limit and pay attention to traffic flow. Anticipate places where cars might slow down to turn or stop. Watch for places motor vehicles merge into traffic. Adjust your speed and direction as needed.

STOP IT

If you're going too fast and want—or need—to come to a complete stop, here are some ways that beat simply jumping off your board:

- Air brake—From a standing position, hold out both arms perpendicular to the body to create air resistance. Air braking is fine for cruising around. However it's less effective than carving and sliding. So, it's not the best choice in an emergency.
- Foot brake—To use a foot brake, lift one foot from the board and gradually place it on the street while balancing on the board with the other foot.
- Sit brake—This is a different kind of foot brake. From a standing position, the rider crouches and then sits on the board while placing both feet on the road.

Foot brakes and sit brakes are good to use when there is too little room for a slide. However, foot braking is hard on the soles of your skate shoes, so use it sparingly.

CONTROLLING SPEED

Before taking your first longboard ride, learn to control your speed and how to stop. Carving is the most important way to control your speed and improve balance on a longboard. Carving is a way to create an "S" pattern in your ride. The rider alternates shifting body weight from the heels to the toes.

To learn the skill, find a parking lot or wide driveway with a slight incline. Push off downhill with the back foot. When you have a bit of speed, bend your knees slightly and shift your weight so the toes point to the sky and heels point to the ground. This action is called heel carving. Keep going until you ride out your speed. Go back to the top of the slant and try toe carving by slightly bending the knees and shifting body weight to the balls of the feet with toes pointed to the ground.

Two longboarders take a ride down a gentlely declining road in a wooded area. Remote places without traffic are best for getting acclimated.

Finally try combining the two types of carving to create an "S" pattern in your "wake." Practice enough to feel comfortable with the movement. Then try carving on steeper and steeper hills until you master the skill. Try wide carves to skate slowly. Try smaller curves to ride faster.

A longboarder does a slide with one hand touching the pavement—in this case, he is doing a speed check.

SLIDE GUIDE

Sliding is another way to slow down, especially if you're traveling faster than you can run. To slide, the rider turns the board sideways so the wheels slide against the ground instead of roll. This motion creates friction, rubbing the wheels against the surface of the concrete to slow down.

Longboarders can perform a slide in any body position, from upright without touching the ground to a crouch with one or both hands touching the pavement. A slide is called a speed check when used to slow down. When used to stop, it's called a shutdown slide. Sliding is the most effective way to slow down or stop completely.

However, sliding is more than a braking mechanism. It has become an element of various tricks. For instance, a pendulum slide is one where the board turns more than 90 degrees and then returns to its first position. The Coleman slide, named for professional skater Cliff Coleman, is a popular hands-down slide that rotates the board 180 degrees with one hand on the ground. Longboarders ride out the Coleman slide to a complete stop.

Challenging slides that require technical skills are used in freeride and dancing (freestyle) longboarding. As more slides are invented, though, they contribute to the developing evolution of sliding as its own type of longboarding. Various slides require wheels of different durometers, so check online or ask skateboard dealers or manufacturers what's best for the tricks you want to learn (see chapters four and five).

CHAPTER THREE

ROAD TRIPS

When you've got someplace to go, your longboard can take you there. In fact, transportation is the main purpose of a longboard. Many riders skate relatively short distances from home to school or work. However, some use their longboards for long-distance skating, called treks.

Commuting is regular travel from one place to another, such as from home to school or work. Longboarders who commute use different board designs, from long, wide cruisers to shorter boards. Many commuters prefer shorter boards between 24 inches and 35 inches (61 to 89 cm) long and medium-size wheels with diameters between 2.5 inches and 3 inches (65 and 75 millimeters), which help smooth out the effects of bumps, cracks, and other obstacles.

Commuters also like loose trucks for sharper turns. Some like kicktails on the deck to make turning on sidewalks easy. They also give the rider a way to lift the toe of the board to jump off a curb.

PUMP IT UP

Commuters use two ways to pick up speed on the road. The first is pushing, which is balancing with one foot on the board while the other foot scoots along the ground. The other is pumping. When a rider picks up enough speed as a result of pushing or riding down a hill, pumping increases speed. Pumping is done by bending the knees and shifting body weight with both feet on the board. The technique resembles the pumping motion on a surfboard. Pumping is easiest to learn on a longboard with loose, tight-turning trucks.

Pushing and pumping are both used in all styles of long-boarding. Pumping on a trek is called long-distance skateboard pumping (LDP). Long-distance rides can cover hundreds or even thousands of miles. Pumping is less tiring than pushing for long-distance travel over a sustained distance.

Pushing is a good technique for gaining speed for short bursts of longboard riding, but it can be exhausting after an extended run.

THE LONGEST RIDE

As of the beginning of 2016, the world record for the longest journey by skateboard was held by Rob Thomson of New Zealand, according to Guinness World Records. He rode 7,555 miles (12,159 kilometers) from Leysin, Switzerland, to Shanghai, China. The trip took more than a year, from June 24, 2007, to September 28, 2008.

Thomson's route included Germany, Belgium, The Netherlands, and England. He left London and crossed the Atlantic Ocean by sailboat with stops in the Caribbean on his way to the United States. From Key West, Florida, he rode across Mississippi, Alabama, Louisiana, Texas, and Arizona to Los Angles, California. In China, Thomson followed China National Highway 312 from Khorogos in Xinjiang Province to Shanghai, with a 311-mile (500-km) detour through Qinghai Province. The ride ended at People's Square in Shanghai.

THE RIGHT BOARD

Skaters who like the idea of riding longer and farther can use any skateboard or longboard. However, most choose a longer, heavier board with large wheels. Big wheels keep the board moving longer and farther with each push than wheels with shorter diameters.

Long-distance riders often want their decks close to the ground to lower the board's center of gravity. Center of gravity is the point in the body where all of its weight is evenly distributed and balanced. The lower the center of gravity of a moving vehicle, like a car, truck, or longboard with rider, the more stable. Longboards can be modified so the deck is closer to the ground, and that is the choice for long-distance skaters.

One way to lower the deck is to use drop-through mounting holes for the trucks. The holes let the rider or manufacturer mount the truck's baseplates differently from the traditional mount. The traditional way to mount the trucks is called top mount, where the trucks attach to the bottom of the deck. With a drop-through mount, the trucks "drop through" the deck and attach to the top of the board. The lower deck makes pushing and foot braking easier and lessens stress on the hips and lower body, which is a benefit over long distances.

Boards with drop-through mounts may also have cut-out sections to give more clearance between the deck and the

This close-up of a rider displaying her board shows how longboards have trucks mounted differently than regular skateboards.

wheels. This helps avoid wheel bite, which brings the board to a sudden, complete stop and often results in a fall. Wheel bite happens when the rider shifts too much weight to one side of the board causing the underside of the deck to contact the wheel and stop its rotation. To adjust the board to prevent wheel bite the rider can add riser pads or change out the wheels for a smaller size.

A drop-down deck sits well below the truck level and barely clears the road. Again, the lower center of gravity gives a more stable ride. It also reduces stress on the knees and lower back.

GOING THE DISTANCE

Distance longboarding takes many forms, and different skating organizations hold events and races for them. For instance, in 2015 the Raceday Longboard Racing Event was held in Rijswijk, Netherlands. The event was held at the 500-meter (547-yard) round RWV De Spartaan bicycle track. There, longboarders competed in a 500-meter sprint and a 5-kilometer (3-mile) race, as well as a three-person relay. Another Dutch event also held in 2015 was the Haagsche Longboard Half Marathon held in the forested neighborhood of Haagsche in The Hague, Netherlands.

Other distance skating events include the mile, the cross-country trek, and the Ultraskate. Ultraskate is an extreme endurance event. It's a twenty-four-hour race to see who can skate farthest over a measured course. As of the beginning of 2016, the world record for the longest ride in twenty-four hours was set by Rick Pronk and Andrew Andras (also known as "Andy The Machine"), who tied at the too-close-to call finish of the Dutch Summer Solstice Ultraskate on June 21, 2015. They each went 285.7 miles (459.8 km) in twenty-four hours.

CHAPTER FOUR

SLIPPERY SLOPES

Riding down hills adds a fun—and often thrilling—element to a longboard outing or race. The three main types of this kind of ride are freeriding, downhill, and slalom, on your own or in organized events and races.

Freeriding is a relatively new entry into the world of longboarding. So far, it's less organized than downhill racing. It involves tricks and techniques at medium to high speeds. The rider controls speed by foot braking and slides. In fact, some riders call freeriding soft wheel sliding because preferred wheels usually fall in the durometer range of 80A to 86A. Both stand-up and hands down slides are important skills. So are grabs, where the rider holds on to one side of the board to perform such tricks as handstands and airborne feats.

Freeriders often choose drop-through, drop-platform, and top-mount longboards with either flexible or stiff decks. Deck length ranges from 36 inches to 44 inches (91 to 112 cm) long and 8.5 to 10.5 inches (21.5 to 26.7 cm) wide. Riders may add kicktails to both sides of the board for technical slides.

A longboarder gets low and plants his hand to perform a slide. Protective gloves are key to doing many similar longboard tricks to protect your hands from scrapes and cuts.

RIDE THE SLIDE

A wide variety of sliding tricks are used in both freeride and freestyle (see chapter five) longboarding. To learn these and other tricks, search online for YouTube or other tutorial videos with demonstrations and instructions. A few of the most popular moves include the following:

- **Layback slide—From a crouch position grab the front of the board with the downhill hand or use** it to balance as you reach back and touch the ground with the uphill hand as you turn the board sideways. Variation: from the layback slide, push up the body into a backbend while sliding.

- Pressure spin—At slow speed on flat pavement jump off the board while kicking the loose board so it spins in circle, then hop back on.

- 360 slide—While moving forward, without touching the ground with the hands, rotate the board in a complete circle and continue down the hill.

- Soft wheel slide—Soft wheel sliding can be used to slow down or stop in all forms of longboarding, but it is especially good for freeriding. A soft wheel slide slows the board for such moves as a 180 slide or stand-up slide.

THE NEED FOR SPEED

If you like to ride fast with style, downhill longboarding is for you. Downhill is also called speedboarding. It's a high-speed thrill where riders can go as fast as motor vehicles. The idea is to ride as fast as possible while maintaining control. According to Guinness World Records at the beginning of 2016, the fastest skateboard speed in a standing position was 80.74 miles per hour (129.94 kilometers per hour). Mischo Erban set the record on June 18, 2012, in Les Éboulements, Quebec, Canada.

Downhill longboarding requires such skills as air braking, sliding, and drifting. Drifting is a controlled turn using changes and balances of rider weight. In addition, the ability to come to a quick, complete stop is critical. Special equipment for downhill includes drop-through, drop-platform, or top-mount decks made of stiff material. Most are made of wood, particularly maple, Baltic birch, and bamboo. Carbon fiber and pressed or milled aluminum may also be used.

Longboard length for downhill usually ranges between 35 inches and 44 inches (95 to 110 cm). The wheelbase should

A longboarder leans into the curve on a downhill run during the 2008 Jochpass Race in Bas Hindelbang in Bavaria, Germany. Longboarding has gained fans worldwide.

range between 28 inches and 35 inches (71 to 89 cm). Racers usually use the drop-through style for truck mounting, although other styles may be chosen. Downhill boards and freeride boards can be used for both styles of riding. The main difference between them is that downhill boards have a distinct front and back. Freeride boards usually are symmetrical, with no difference between the front and rear. Safety gear for serious racers includes racing leathers, full body suits that protect the rider's skin in a fall.

WHY THE WOBBLE?

At high speeds on steep hills, a longboard reacts to every rider action and weight shift differently from the way it reacts at slower speeds. If the rider over-corrects for the board's surprise movement, his or her longboard may exhibit speed wobbles that threaten the safety and well-being of the rider. In other words, you can take a nasty fall. Speed wobbles may be reduced or eliminated by one of the following methods:

- **Increase the skill level. Before trying a high-speed run, be sure to know how to navigate the grades and difficulties the hill presents.**
- **Replace bushings with ones with a higher durometer.**
- **Tighten the rear truck.**

NIP AND TUCK

Snow ski racers use tucks to reduce air resistance for the fastest speed possible. Downhill racers use them, too, for the same reasons. To perform a tuck, bend the knees as much as possible with the front thigh parallel to the ground. Bend at the waist and place the chest on the thigh. Place the arms in back with hands together. Lean forward and tuck the head lower than the shoulders to create the smallest aerodynamic profile possible.

In the American tuck the rider places the back knee immediately behind the front knee. The rider's back is flat. In a Euro tuck, the back knee is placed behind the front ankle, and the rider's back is curved. A Euro tuck gets the rider closer to the ground but also creates more drag from the chest than the American tuck. A Euro tuck can also be uncomfortable. In a hybrid tuck the rider places the back knee in the middle of the front calf, combining the advantages and disadvantages of both the American and Euro methods.

Drafting is technique downhill racers use to go faster. The rider rides close behind another racer, which lets the forward person take the brunt of wind resistance. The person who is drafting then pops out from behind the other racer at increased speed.

OBSTACLE COURSES

Slalom is another form of longboarding borrowed from snow sports. Alpine skiing and alpine snowboarding both use slalom to weave in and out of poles or gates. Longboard slalom racing first appeared in the 1960s and remained popular into the 1970s. But interest in it declined. In the 2000s, longboarders took it up again.

A longboarder helps put out traffic cones in preparation for a longboard slalom run, one of the styles of longboarding that requires particular speed and dexterity.

In longboard slaloming, riders swerve in and out of obstacles—usually plastic cones—placed a specific distance apart on a hill. The racer tries for the fastest time down the hill but is penalized for each cone knocked down. Another form of slalom is called civilian slalom or pedestrian slalom. It still involves weaving in and out of obstacles, which may include pedestrians. Civilian slalom is not a formal event but rather the way a commuter or other rider weaves in and out along the way.

Wheels for slalomers vary from front to back. The front wheels are slightly harder than the back wheels. The harder wheels reduce resistance from the pavement and let the rider go faster. The back wheels need to be soft so they can grip the pavement through turns. Carving is the main technique slalomers use.

CHAPTER FIVE

SHALL WE DANCE?

Can you Chop the Wood, Walk the Plank, and Pirouette on a longboard? Chances are you're into longboard dancing, also known as boardwalking and freestyling. While downhill is about speed and distance skating is about going places, dancing is about going places with style. The board becomes a dance floor, and the rider moves back and forth on the board while performing a series of technical steps for fun and entertainment. It is the most creative form of longboarding. Tricks rely on balance and foot placement, as well as accuracy.

Dancing is not for newbies. But less experienced riders can enjoy some of the easier moves. First, though, riders need a good feel for their boards and the ability to control them on both hills and level streets. Sliding skills (see chapter four) and use of regular and goofy stances are important techniques to know. A regular stance is standing on the board with the left foot in front. Goofy stance is the opposite. The right foot is forward. Most longboarders are most comfortable with the dominant foot in back. Dancers need to be able to use both stances.

THE RIGHT STUFF

Dancers, like other longboarders, need the right equipment. Decks for this type of longboarding need versatility. The most common boards for dance moves are longer than 48 inches (122 cm). However, some dancers use shorter ones. Dance boards are also wider than those for other longboard styles to give the rider more foot room.

Decks need moderate flexibility to respond well at slow speeds. They need enough bounce for carving but also need firmness for a steady ride. Most dance boards are flat with a slight upward curve in the middle. Others may be concave, which refers to the curve between the front and tail of the deck. A concave board is stronger than a flat one and helps the rider control the ride. Because dancers often ride the board in both directions, a symmetrical deck with twin kicktails is best.

So are drop-through truck mounts. The best choice for trucks is the 180 millimeter size for good stability and responsive turns. Wheels for dancing tend to have a durometer higher than 90A for hard wheel sliding. Hard wheel sliding is for technical riding where style

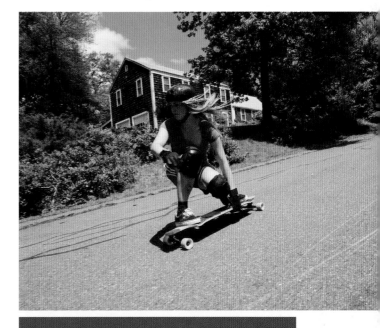

A woman speeds down a suburban road with a concave longboard.

is more important than speed. Hard wheels let the rider perform aggressive slides for more precision.

STEP BY STEP

Freestyle skateboarders in the past developed a number of jumps and other tricks that involve flipping the skateboard. However longboard dancers don't rely on them. Such skateboard tricks as the Ollie, where the rider pops the front of the board, jumps, and lands on the board are too "ordinary" for longboard dancing.

A good dancing trick to try first is Chop the Wood. Balance on the board with one foot while holding the other out front. Then hop on the first foot. A more difficult move is called Walk the Plank. The rider "simply" walks back and forth on the board while the board is in motion. In the Pirouette, the rider lifts the back foot and pivots in a complete circle on the ball of the front foot, then returns the back foot to the board. The Pirouette can be combined with Walk the Plank for increased style.

Another trick on the easier end of the scale is the Lookback. The rider suddenly changes direction. To perform the Lookback, drop one foot

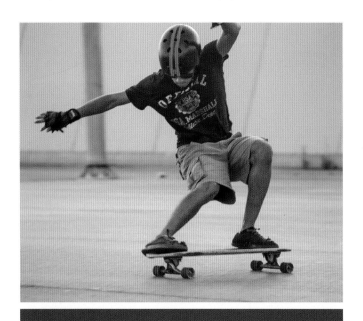

Once you have gained enough confidence on the longboard to move around easily, the next step is to learn some tricks and get creative.

onto the ground. Push the board forward and bring it to a sudden stop by pressing the heel of the other foot onto the board's edge. Jump back onto the board with both feet, but turn the body 180 degrees before landing.

WHAT'D YOU SAY?

Longboarders have developed a language all their own. If you're new to longboarding, learning these slang words can help you communicate with others.

bail **Fall off the board.**

bomb **Zoom downhill.**

Dad **A word used as a name for other skaters or just something to say.**

eat it **Crash.**

high side **A forward downhill fall caused by wheel bite in the middle of a slide.**

low side **A situation where the board shoots out from under the rider.**

mobbing **Skating really, really fast.**

shralpping **Skating in a way that's even better than shredding**

shredding **Skating in an way that proves one's skill.**

steeze **A combination of style and ease; coolness.**

thane lines **The marks on pavement made by sliding with urethane wheels.**

throw down **An awesome trick performed exceptionally well.**

trill **A combination of "true" and "real" meaning "cool."**

LEARNING NEW MOVES

More advanced dance steps include the Shanker, Cross-step, and Peter Pan. The Shanker is similar to Walk the Plank. It's a turn where the rider stands in the middle of the board and steps toward the end. He or she then lifts the front of the board by pressing on the other end. With the end of the board in the air, the rider turns his or her body in a half circle stopping in the middle of the board.

Longboard dancing borrowed the Cross-step directly from ocean surfing. Cross-stepping resembles Walking the Plank. However the rider crosses his or her legs while moving along the board. Start with feet perpendicular to the direction of travel. Place the front foot in the middle of the board. Cross the back foot over the front foot. Then move the foot that was just crossed behind the crossing foot to the front of the board. Move the other foot to the back of the board so the feet are wide apart. Then return the foot that was crossed to its original position on the middle of the board. You can also do the Cross-step by crossing the back foot behind the front foot for a slightly more difficult trick. Combining Cross-steps with Walk the Plank and other moves gives you a ride with style.

The Peter Pan is similar to the Cross-step, except the feet point in the direction of travel in the middle of the board. To begin place the feet in the goofy stance with the right foot in front and both feet perpendicular to the direction of travel. Pick up the right foot and place its inner edge on the outside left edge of the board facing forward. Cross the left foot over the right foot and place the inner edge of the left foot on the far right side edge of the board. Now move the right foot behind the left and cross over the left foot to the original position.

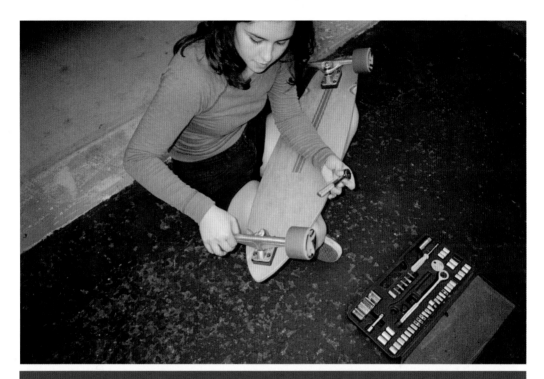

A longboarder breaks out her tool kit to tighten up the trucks on her board. Longboarders often espouse a do-it-yourself (DIY) approach. Boarders often modify and innovate with their boards, too.

To learn these tricks and others, ask a friend to teach you. Or, search the Internet for videos that include demonstration and instruction of the moves you want to learn. Practice first on the ground. Then try it on the board with the board motionless on a lawn or piece of ground where it won't slip out from under you. You might find it helpful to break down the move into several parts until you master each segment of the step. Practice on the street at slow speeds until you're comfortable with the movement. Once you have several dance steps under your belt, make up some of your own. Try adapting dance floor steps to the board. Improvise. Anything goes. That's what longboard dancing is all about.

GLOSSARY

air brake A way to slow down or stop by holding out the arms perpendicular to the body to increase wind resistance.

blind curve A turn in the road where neither the rider nor an oncoming car driver can see what's ahead.

boardwalking Another name for dancing and freestyling.

carving Turning back and forth down a hill. Can be used to control speed and come to a stop.

dancing Also known as freestyling or boardwalking, the use of a longboard as a dance floor, using various steps to move back and forth on the board.

deck The longboard or skateboard platform.

downhill A form of longboarding where riders seek to achieve the highest speed possible while maintaining control of the board.

drafting In downhill racing, taking advantage of another rider's windbreak to increase speed and popping out to pass the other person.

drifting A controlled turn resulting from changes and balances of rider weight.

durometer A measure of hardness of bushings and wheels.

footbrake A way to slow down or stop by keeping one foot on the board and slowly placing the other on the ground and dragging the foot, sole down.

freeriding A form of downhill skateboarding that uses tricks and technical moves and medium to high speeds.

freestyling A form of longboarding also known as dancing or boardwalking.

goofy stance Standing on a board with the right foot in front and both feet perpendicular to the direction of travel.

pushing A way to propel a board by keeping one foot on the deck and using the other to scoot along the roadway and pick up speed.

pumping A way to shift the rider's weight through a series of balanced turns to increase speed while keeping both feet on the board.

racing leathers Full body suit that protects the rider's skin in a fall.

regular stance Standing on the board with the left foot in front.

shutdown slide A slide used to come to a complete stop, usually at the end of a hill.

slalom A form of longboarding where riders weave in and out of obstacles in races or on the street or sidewalk.

slide A method of longboard riding where the rider turns the wheels perpendicular to the direction of travel in order to slow down or stop.

speed check A slide used to slow down.

speed wobble An unexpectant movement by a longboard at high speeds that results from the rider overreacting to his or her move or weight shift.

trek A long-distance longboard ride.

truck The axle that the longboard wheels rotate around.

The A.skate Foundation
2612 Woodfern Court
Birmingham, AL 35209
Website http://www.askate.org
With the motto, "Skating with kids through acceptance, therapy, and education," the A.skate Foundation organizes clinics to teach children with autism the basic skills of skateboarding. A.skate is based in Birmingham, Alabama, and has programs in numerous cities throughout the United States, as well as Ireland, Guam, and Australia.

International Association of Skateboard Companies (IASC)
315 S. Coast Hwy 101, Suite U-253
Encinitas, CA 92024
(949) 455-1112
Website: http://theiasc.org
IASC is an organization of skateboard manufacturers, distributors, contest organizers, private skate parks, and individuals that represents skateboarders and the skateboard industry to promote the sport.

International Skateboarding Federation
P.O. Box 57
Woodward, PA 16882
(814) 883-5635

Website: http://www.internationalskateboardingfederation.com
The International Skateboarding Federation (ISF) is the world
governing body for the sport of skateboarding with the goals
of making skateboarding available worldwide and promoting
the sport.

Longboarding for Peace
1136 Center Street
Suite 293
Thornhill, ON L4J 3M8
Canada
(416) 807-0805
E-mail: mbrooke@interlog.com
Website: http://www.longboardingforpeace.org
The goal of Longboarding for Peace is to create a worldwide
"Peace Army" of fifty thousand longboarders who pledge to
perform at least one act of kindness each day.

SkateAcrossUSA
Ari Mannis
3525 Del Mar Heights Road, #231
San Diego, CA 92130
(619) 940-6508
E-mail: info@skateacrossusa.com
Website: http://skateacrossusa.com/contact-us
SkateAcrossUSA is a nonprofit organization that raises money for
charitable causes by holding long-distance skating events in
the United States.

Tony Hawk Foundation
1611-A S. Melrose Drive, #360
Vista, CA 92081
(760) 477-2479
E-mail: information@tonyhawk.com
Website: http://tonyhawkfoundation.org
The Tony Hawk Foundation supports the building of public skateboard parks in low-income communities in the United States and other countries as a way to support and encourage youth and improve society.

Vancouver Skateboarding Coalition
c/o Antisocial
2337 Main Street
Vancouver, BC V5T 3C9
Canada
(604) 708-5678
Website: http://www.vsbc.ca
The Vancouver Skateboarding Coalition serves as Vancouver's "voice for skateboarding." It promotes unity among the city's skateboarders and encourages safe, fun environments for the sport.

WEBSITES

Because of the changing number of Internet links, Rosen Publishing has developed an online list of websites related to the subject of this book. This site is updated regularly. Please use this link to access this list:

http://www.rosenlinks.com/STT/long

Adamson, Thomas K. *Big Air Skateboarding.* Minneapolis, MN: Bellwether Media, 2015.

Adamson, Thomas K. *Skateboarding Street Style.* Minneapolis, MN: Bellwether Media, 2015.

Beal, Becky. *Skateboarding: The Ultimate Guide.* Santa Barbara, CA: Greenwood, 2013.

Berger, Matt. *The Handmade Skateboard Design & Build a Custom Longboard, Cruiser, or Street Deck from Scratch.* Nashville, TN:, Spring House Press, 2014.

Castellano, Peter. *Longboard Skateboarding* (Daredevil Sports). New York, NY: Gareth Stevens Publishing, 2015.

Christie, Michael. *If I Fall, If I Die: A Novel.* New York, NY: Hogarth, 2015.

Cliver, Sean. *The Disposable Skateboard Bible.* Berkeley, CA: Gingko Press, 2009.

Committee on Sports-Related Concussions in Youth, et al. *Sports-Related Concussions in Youth: Improving the Science, Changing the Culture.* Washington, DC: National Academies Press, 2014.

Fitzpatrick, Jim. *Skateboarding.* Vero Beach, FL: Rourke Educational Media, 2015.

Herrera, Juan Felipe. *SkateFate.* New York, NY: HarperTeen, 2015.

Maddox, Jake. *Skateboard Idol.* North Mankato, MN: Stone Arch Books, 2016.

Mehring, Jonathan, and Tony Hawk. *Skate the World: Photographing One World of Skateboarding,* Des Moines, IA: National Geographic, 2015.

Nixon, James. *Skateboarding Champion* (How to Be a Champion). London, England: Franklin Watts Ltd., 2015.

Parnavelas, Ellen. *Long Live South Bank.* London, England: Heni Publishing, 2015.

Quartersnacks. *TF at 1: 10 Years of Quartersnacks.* Brooklyn, NY: Powerhouse Books, 2015.

Rajczak, Kristen. *Skateboarding* (Sports to the Extreme). New York, NY: Rosen Publishing, 2015.

Stutt, Ryan. *Skateboarding Skills: Everything a New Rider Needs to Know.* Buffalo, NY: Firefly Books, 2014.

Toole, Nikki. *Skater.* Heidelberg, Germany: Kehrer Verlag, 2015.

Welinder, Per, and Pete Whitley. *Mastering Skateboarding.* Champaign, IL: Human Kinetics, 2011.

Werner, Doug, and Steve Badillo. *Skateboarding: Book of Tricks.* Huntingdon, Cambridgeshire, England: Track Publishing, 2015.

BIBLIOGRAPHY

Beginner Longboarding. "Beginner Longboarding Tips" (http://beginnerlongboarding.com/beginner-longboarding-tips/).

Cave, Steve. "Advanced Longboarding—Longboard Dancing Trick Tips." About Sports, December 15, 2014 (http://skateboard.about.com/od/fringeboarding/a/LongboardDancin.htm).

Chandler, Mischa. "Skate Safe Manifesto." Rayne.com (http://www.rayne.com/skate-safe/).

Conspiracy Skateboard. "Tutorial Peter Pan Longboard." YouTube.com, February 8, 2014 (https://www.youtube.com/watch?v=Z6FJELyA_pY).

Guinness World Records. "Longest Journey by Skateboard." 2015 (http://www.guinnessworldrecords.com/world-records/longest-journey-by-skateboard).

"How to Slide on a Longboard for Beginners." YouTube.com, September 1, 2013 (https://www.youtube.com/watch?v=BZAzrFF5emE).

Huntington, Scott. "The History of Longboarding." February 10, 2014 (http://sportsthenandnow.com/2014/02/10/the-history-of-longboarding/).

Muirskate.com. "Longboard Buying Guide." 2015 (https://www.muirskate.com/longboard-guide/dictionary).

Polydoros, Lori. *Skateboarding Greats*. Mankato, MN: Capstone Press, 2012.

Robertson, Les. "New Ultraskate Long Distance Push World Record." Skateslate.com, August 5, 2015 (http://www.skateslate.com/blog/2015/08/05/new-ultraskate-long-distance-push-world-record).

The Stoked Team. "Longboard Lingo—The Complete Guide to Longboard Slang" (https://stokedskateboards.com/knowledge-base/longboard-slang.html).

Styleboard. "Longboard Dancing Step 06 Chop Series." YouTube.com, May 22, 2014 (https://www.youtube.com/watch?v=kSj9N9DnMCc).

Tactics.com. "Longboarding Essentials" (http://www.tactics.com/info/longboarding).

Tadlock, Lindsay. "The History of Longboarding." Livestrong, June 23, 2015 (http://www.livestrong.com/article/351382-the-history-of-longboarding/#sthash.qoXXcoj2.dpuf).

"Tutorial longboard #2—Layback slide." YouTube, January 28, 2013 (https://www.youtube.com/watch?v=yODp3U8FWrw).

Varca, Louis. "How to Longboard Dance." Mademan.com, July 7, 2010 (http://www.mademan.com/mm/how-longboard-dance.html#ixzz3tBvkqNpk).

Warehouse Skateboards. "What Size Skateboard Do I Need?" November 23, 2011 (https://www.warehouseskateboards.com/blog/2011/11/23/what-size-skateboard-do-i-need/).

Wippermann, Max. "How to: Tucking on a Longboard." Motion Board Shop (http://www.motionboardshop.com/pages/how-to-tucking-on-a-longboard).

INDEX

ABOUT THE AUTHOR

Mary-Lane Kamberg is the author of *Kawasaki: World's Fastest Bike*, *North Carolina Basketball*, *Saltwater Fishing*, and *Sports Concussions*. She has also written about sports topics for *Current Health* and *Swimming World* magazines. She lives in Olathe, Kansas.

PHOTO CREDITS

Cover Christian Aslund/Lonely Planet Images/Getty Images; pp. 1, 6, 13, 20, 25, 32 Tupungato/Shutterstock.com; p. 3 Dizzo/Vetta/Getty Images; pp. 4-5 mgs/Moment Open/Getty Images; pp. 5 (inset), 9 Darryl Leniuk/The Image Bank/Getty Images; p. 7 William Andrew/Moment/Getty Images; p. 11 Rick Madonik/Toronto Star/Getty Images; p. 15 Forest Woodward/E+/Getty Images; pp. 17, 18-19 Daniel Milchev/Stone/Getty Images; p. 21 vaquey/Moment/Getty Images; p. 23 Peathegee Inc./Blend Images/Getty Images; p. 26 © GraficallyMinded/Alamy Stock Photo; p. 28 © imageBROKER/Alamy Stock Photo; p. 31 © NearTheCoast.com/Alamy Stock Photo; p. 33 Meg Haywood-Sullivan/Getty Images; p. 34 Artur Debat/Moment Mobile/Getty Images; p. 37 Stephanie Noritz/Taxi/Getty Images; back cover, interior pages (bricks) Ensuper/Shutterstock.com; interior pages banner textures Naburalna/Shutterstock.com

Designer: Michael Moy; Editor: Philip Wolny;
Photo Researcher: Karen Huang and Philip Wolny